For You,

Alexander Evans

BookLeaf
Publishing

Presentation by *BookLeaf Publishing*

Web: www.bookleafpub.com

E-mail: info@bookleafpub.com

ISBN: 978-93-95755-27-6

First edition 2022

*Dedicated to all of you that find a piece of
yourself within these pages.*

ACKNOWLEDGEMENT

I would like to acknowledge the Kaurna people who are the traditional custodians of the land on which I read and write. I pay my respects to their elders past and present and recognise that this land always was, and always will be Aboriginal land.

I would also like to acknowledge my mother and my brother, who have been with me on my writing journey since the moment I laid my first word onto paper. I can never truly tell you how deeply grateful I am for your love.

PREFACE

The purpose of this collection is to share the way I see life, the experiences I have lived, and thoughts that have never left my brain. I hope, perhaps that they will inspire you to create something magnificent, to tell someone you love them, or simply appreciate life for all the great things it can offer you.

Once you have finished reading, I ask that you find something small, that you have never noticed before and be aware of the joy it gives you. Like tasting the rain or the smell of oranges.

For You, A Mirror

A Universe inside your eyes.
It contains nothing yet everything.
In the deepest black, the empty space between,
Is speckles of light, speckles of life.
The sparkles distract and intrigue,
Drawing in like a hook on a fishing line,
Pulling you in with no mercy.

And in that inevitability comes a glimmer,
Of anticipation, of mystery.
The idea that each speckle;
Like dust upon a surface,
Has the potential to be something infinite,
Something explosive.

Filled with wonder,
Each white, silvery flicker has its own story
Another infinite, ever-expanding exposé on a
life
One long lived in the moment, yet barely just
begun.
The sheer amount that exists in the smallest
section
Is unfathomable, yet strangely comforting

These flickers.
These moments;
Are never-ending,
Looping forever on a stream of their own
existence.

And each flicker contains you, and only you.
For you are the universe, the everything, and the
nothing.
The all-encompassing and the dead silent.
You, the mirror into my own desires,
My own fears.
My own deepest levels I knew not exist.

When you stand silent, the world stops.
When you smile, each and every star in the
universe burns bright.
When you breathe, the planets do too.
The stars retract and the galaxies are calm.

All of this is because of you.
You. The Universe.
All-encompassing and ever contained
Within one body; a vessel,
Within one mind; a consciousness,
Within one beauty; You.

For you, A Mirror

A Cosmic Haiku

Black sky, full of stars.
Hello - Is anyone there?
Nothing. Then response.

A Lover, Ages Ago

She was the first girl to say "I love you."
But that love was not endless,
So when it had spilled out and dried up,
She was the first girl to say "I hate you."

There Is An Eyelash In My Brain

There is an eyelash in my brain,
The back left corner is where it lay.

It pokes, and prods, and breeds discomfort.
To rid this blight would be triumphant.

I feel it there, in my grey matter,
If it is death or acceptance I prefer the latter.

I have learned to accept the pain,
There is an eyelash in my brain.

Comfort Zone

A house is a home when a home is a music box.
It plays a song of memories, each time it
unlocks.
Melodies of laughter,
Rhythm of smiles,
Perhaps I'll sit and listen awhile.

A house is a home when a home is a hospital.
Ready to patch you up each time that you fall.
A mother, a nurse, with soup when you're sick.
Or band-aids for scratches when playing with
sticks.

A house is a home when a home is a cradle.
Ready to swaddle when you are not able.
Walls of protection to stop you from falling,
Or to comfort your soul when the sadness comes
calling.

A house is a home when a home is a heart.
Filled with love, right from the start.
Family and friends and a place to meet.
To have a chat, while you rest your feet.

So thank you home, for all that you are,
You are a warming hearth and a guiding star.

Land Of The White Dog

I scutter and run, chasing at ankles.
And hear mouths protrude foreign words.
Inside I walk underneath chairs and tables,
Outside I yell at trespassing birds.

I eat the same breakfast every morning,
And a thrown treat, from the table above.
Each time I eat, my taste buds are adoring,
Tasting better from the hand of the owner I love.

Sometimes I wish I could hear them talk,
And understand the words they say.
Like when taking them for a walk,
I wish I could take them every day.

When we are together they mimic my smile.
I have so many things I want to say.
Like when they leave me and are gone for a
while.
I want to tell them I wish they could stay.

They treat me like royalty when they are at
home,
A castle to sleep, drink, cuddle and eat.
I have whatever I want, whether a bone,
Or liver or a throne for a seat.

They are a chef, a chauffeur, and a hairdresser.
A trainer, a servant, the list does not end.
But from someone who loves me, I'd expect no
lesser.
Because man is family and a dog's best friend.

A Conversation Of Love

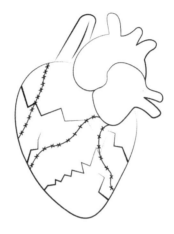

I met a girl that I once knew,
She use to speak of heartbreak too.
She told me of a boy once gone,
Whose heart had leathered and worn.
It was nothing sinister, malicious, or grim.
She had just fallen out of love with him.

Ode To A Machine

Metal of history, swords, and typewriters,
And watches and bikes and cigarette lighters.
These analog, mechanical, cordless machines,
That most people think, their time has been.
Perhaps that is true, for those listed above,
Except for the second that has found a new love.

I can take it with me when I want to write,
On cozy Sunday morning, or productive
Wednesday night.
When there is no need for a buzzing screen,
Or a hole in the wall where power is gleaned.

Each press of the key is writing on history,
The previous owner as much of a mystery,
As the words of the page when those keys were
first pressed.
Where perhaps a young woman, failed her
typing test.

Though it may be heavy and old,
And made of metal that absorbs the cold.
I like my typewriter like a new friend,
I hope it is there when my poem comes to an
end.

A Sin

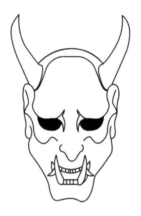

Gone below the hearts of men,
Recognised only once it has reared its ugly head,
Exists an evil that will not stop,
Even when all has been claimed.
Demanding more, always demanding.
Like taking three lovers, or flying for the sun.
It asks again,
Expecting you to listen.
"Silence"! you must tell the foul beast, and all
will be quiet once again.

Rest In Peace

These 14 hours have been hell for you,
And the tears build now as your time is due.
Your grip goes limp as your skin fades,
And your mind has returned to better days.

It was two months of escape,
But I had to give in to my fate.

So the escape that I was trying to pursue,
Could not save me from the chaos that would
ensue.
When I let myself feel,
Everything that I was trying to kill.

So when I look up at the night and watch your
smile gleam.
Crying under the stars is not as lonely as it
seems.

Ode To Home

Beaches of sand, shine like a billion stars,
Catching up after years long passed.
They stretch as far as you can see,
The coast littered with jetty's wooden beams.

On the melting hot, summer days,
Beads of sweat are prayers to the golden sun
rays.
In the winter, the wind blows wrinkles to make
your bones cold.
It breathes on everything and makes it feel old.

An endless hustle and bustle of shoppers,
And workers in stores become eavesdroppers.

Only endless from Friday morning to Sunday night,
Where the city of churches is covered in light.

On the coast, the white gulls are soaring,
On hot January evenings, and cold July mornings.
Where they dive for chips covered in vinegar.
Or remnants of donuts, with cinnamon sugar.

To a tourist, maybe it won't look like much,
Maybe a fringe or balls or a pig they can touch.
Of course, there are streets, like Rundle and Hindley,
Where people will seek when they want their night lively.

Perhaps in the mid-year, there is a desire to leave,
When the chilling cold wind causes a cough and a sneeze.
But when I am gone and feeling alone.
I know I'll have this place to call home.

So when I am old and bitter and jaded,
And my soul has left and my skin has faded.
Someone will ask where I should be laid.
You tell them in his home of Adelaide.

Rejection Is Power

There are those out there,
who will feel it necessary to tell you how to live
your life.
Who will say that you should do what they do,
the way they have done.

To reject their words, and follow your own, is a
true demonstration of strength.
Because when you are armed with your own
self-path,
Your own desire to live your life, their words
will mean nothing.
Like a bug informing you on how to build a
house.

A Frequent Visitor

Grief is like an old friend who moved away to the next town over.

One who visits every now and then, without warning, to remind you of all the times you spent together.

They will leave and you will hear them in your mind until enough time has passed and their words fade again.

But just like they always do, they will come back, on their own accord, and you will feel obliged to give them the time they deserve even though you now have your own life to live.

My favourite Book

You are my favourite book,
When there is nothing else to read, I open you.
Each turn of the page reveals new secrets,
Each word is a tattoo on your flesh,
Each letter I read screams your name.
The scent of the pages comforts me.
But it is time to finally put you down, and read a
new book.

A Powerful Word

Like a chain wrapped 'round a neck,
Or pulling on one's hair.
A word tells you that you've left,
Almost but not quite there.
It is made of three letters,
alone it is but bare,
But when it is with a sentence
It pulls up on the hair.

"I do not love you," says the girl to the boy in tow.
But with the word tacked on the end his hope will only grow.
So that boy will follow still,
And he will not forget,
That word tacked on the end of hers,
"I do not love you...yet"

Remember That You Will Die

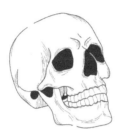

When you find yourself, taking another shift or selling your favourite toy from your childhood, Memento Mori.

When you are shedding tears on the bathroom floor, because they found someone else, Memento Mori.

When you are chasing that high, reaching for the
next pipe, the next syringe, the next vein,
Memento Mori.

When you lay on your deathbed, surrounded by
your loved ones or by no one at all, Memento
Mori.

When all you have done, is concern yourself
with the dollar, the jewellery, the job,
And it all comes crashing down and life has
robbed you of those things,
You will look out from your cardboard box, at
the pressed suits and gold rings. Memento Mori.

L - - E

Life and Love.
Interchangeable, mirrors of each other.
For to love is to live,
And to live is lovely.

Square Hole Into Everything

First, it was a screen in the living room,
Then a screen on the fridge.
Now there's a screen in your child's plan,
What comes next? A screen in their head?

Countdown To Heartbreak

Ten - the number on the clock the first time we met, nine sacred words whispered in my ear. we sat on the beach and ate pizza, no mind to chewing sand.
Seven hours later still holding hands/omely dressed, elegant style, it's what you dreamed of when you were six.
Five - the number of times we kissed, each time the collision of our lips masked the question of what I was there for was that you needed someone to talk to at three in the morning, when you were too drunk to remember my name but not his. How stupid I was to think you were the one.
Back to square zero.

A Letter To A Dragon

Dear Father Time,
You do not know me, I am but a mere speck of
dust on your infinite body,
But I know you all too well.

Some have called you a tyrant, for you have
taken countless souls, stood idly by and watched
civilisations rise and fall in the blink of an eye,
and looked on as the world has grown
cancerous.

Others have called you a gift-giver, for you have brought new life, delivered treasured memories, and provided unfathomable, infinite, knowledge.

Sometimes I wonder if you know what you have done.

I have spent much of my life thinking about you, your callous nature, your idle disrespect, your infinite existence. I have tried being you too, standing, watching, not interfering in the matters of life. But I can wait no longer.

You have taken too much from me now, and I will never get back what I have lost to your godly power.

All I can do is submit.

Sincerely,
Your loyal servant,
Humanity

A Mirror, For You

Hello, you, majestic beast.

You who has completed so much, accomplished such great feats, yet still does not recognise it.

You who does not recognise your own awe-inspiring amazement, simply through your own existence.

Though you started as a single cell, the sheer beauty, that you, dear reader, have come this far, to where you are in this very moment, is a triumph.

For you started as a small being, created from the love of two others and look at all you have accomplished. All of the people you have loved, and the heartbreak you have felt. All of the tears you have shed and the smiles you have bred. All of the beauty that exists in your eyes and the beauty seen through them.

With all of your infinite experience and personal wisdom, you still call yourself not good enough, still doubt your ability, still fear the things that cannot hurt you.

The only thing you need in this world replete with beauty is you.

This poem is a mirror, for you.

But a poem, cannot provide you meaning in your life.
A poem cannot give you purpose to continue onwards.
A poem cannot give you the motivation to achieve all the great things you are already capable of doing.

That, dear reader, is for you to do.

Ingram Content Group UK Ltd.
Milton Keynes UK
UKHW021105310323
419467UK00016B/721

9 789395 755276